The Fall of
The House of Usher

*A Gothic Descent into Madness,
Ancestral Decay & the Terrifying
Unknown*

A Modern Translation
Adapted for the Contemporary Reader

Edgar Allan Poe

Translated by Tim Zengerink

Table of Contents

Preface
Message to the Reader

Rebuilding the Greatest Library in Human History

Thousands of years ago, the Library of Alexandria was the heart of global knowledge — a sanctuary where the wisdom of every known civilization was gathered and shared freely.

And then, it was lost.

Now, we're rebuilding it — and you are invited to join us.

At the Library of Alexandria, we've set out to make every book available to every person on Earth — not just in print, but in every language, every format, and for every reader.

Here's how we do it:

- **Deluxe Print Editions at True Printing Cost** - Order any book as a high-quality paperback, elegant hardcover, or stunning boxset — and only pay what it costs to print. No markups. No middlemen.
- **Unlimited Access to the Greatest Works** - Enjoy thousands of timeless classics — from Plato to Shakespeare to Tolstoy — in beautiful, modern eBook and audiobook editions. Read and listen without limits — for every reader, everywhere.
- **Modern Translations for Every Language & Dialect** - We're reimagining the classics in clear, accessible language — and translating them into every dialect imaginable. Everyone deserves to understand humanity's greatest ideas.

When you visit **LibraryofAlexandria.com**, you're not just accessing books — you're joining a global movement to restore, preserve, and share the wisdom of civilization.

Join us today at LibraryofAlexandria.com

Together, we'll ensure the light of human wisdom never fades again.

With gratitude,

The Modern Library of Alexandria Team

Visit:
www.libraryofalexandria.com
Or scan the code below:

Introduction

Madness, Mortality,
and the Haunted Psyche

Few stories in American literature plunge so directly into the darkness of the human mind and the terror of disintegration as Edgar Allan Poe's *The Fall of the House of Usher*. First published in 1839, this short story stands as a towering achievement in Gothic fiction, weaving a tale of psychological dread, supernatural suggestion, and metaphysical collapse that continues to haunt readers nearly two centuries later. With its decaying mansion, eerie twins, and unnamed narrator, the story is not merely about physical ruin, but about the collapse of identity, reason, and reality itself.

Poe was a master of mood, and *The Fall of the House of Usher* is perhaps his most perfect creation in terms of atmosphere. From the first sentence to the final cataclysmic fall, the narrative pulls the reader into a world ruled by shadow, silence, and psychological unease. The story's landscape—a remote and desolate region, a mansion crumbling from within, a tarn reflecting a distorted world—is not merely setting but symbol, reflecting the inner decay of its central figure, Roderick Usher, and the doomed lineage he represents.

The narrator, whose name is never revealed, arrives at the House of Usher at the behest of his childhood friend Roderick, who is suffering from what he calls a "nervous affliction" of the most oppressive kind. What he finds is a world untethered from logic and vitality. Roderick, pale and hypersensitive, lives in fear and isolation with his twin sister Madeline, who herself suffers from a mysterious illness and is wasting away before his eyes. As the story unfolds, Madeline dies—or appears to—and is entombed beneath the house. But the climax reveals that she was buried alive, and her return, bleeding and broken, leads to the literal and symbolic collapse of the Usher house.

This tale is not a simple ghost story. Rather, it is a profound allegory about the fragility of the human mind, the inherited weight of familial guilt, and the uncanny connection between environment and psyche. The "house" is not just a building; it is a body, a mind, a bloodline. Its fall is not just architectural—it is existential. Poe's tale functions as an extended meditation on what happens when identity is cut off from the world, when isolation becomes madness, and when reality begins to devour itself from the inside.

Decay and Doubling:
Gothic Traditions and Poe's Innovations

The Fall of the House of Usher emerges from the rich tradition of Gothic literature, a genre rooted in 18th-century England and marked by settings of gloom, themes of terror, and a fascination with the supernatural. But Poe, writing in a young America, infused the genre with uniquely psychological depth. He was less interested in ghosts than in the ghostly dimensions of the mind—less in external horrors than in internal disintegration.

The theme of "doubling" is central to the tale. Roderick and Madeline are not merely siblings—they are twins, mirror images of one another, sharing not just a family but a fate. Their identities are so intertwined that the death of one inevitably means the death of the other. Critics have long interpreted Madeline as the physical embodiment of Roderick's repressed fears, desires, or illness—his doppelgänger, his unconscious, or even his soul. The narrator, a rational outsider, stands at first as a counterpoint to this closed system, but even he is drawn into its logic, unable to resist the spell of the house and the family within.

Poe builds his world with an obsessive attention to detail. The crack in the mansion's façade seen upon the narrator's arrival foreshadows the ultimate collapse—an external representation of the internal fracture. The tarn reflects a distorted image of the house, suggesting the blurred line between perception and reality. The oppressive atmosphere, the dim corridors, the strange sounds in the night—all serve to erode the boundaries between the real and the imagined. This technique is not mere decoration but essential to Poe's design: terror, for him, arises from the destabilization of the known.

The power of the story lies not in what is explained, but in what is left unexplained. Is Madeline a ghost, a revenant, a hallucination? Is the house itself alive, a sentient structure feeding off its inhabitants? Poe does not answer these questions, and that ambiguity is part of the tale's terror. By refusing to offer a firm resolution, Poe leaves the reader suspended in uncertainty, forced to confront the possibility that the greatest horrors are those that dwell within the mind.

The story also plays with the idea of inheritance—genetic, psychological, and architectural. The Usher family is described as having no offshoots; their bloodline is insular, self-contained, and self-consuming. The house, too, has been passed down through generations, becoming not just a dwelling but a repository of madness. This recursive structure—people trapped in a house, the house trapped in their minds—creates a claustrophobic effect that intensifies with each page. Poe suggests that when a lineage turns inward, unchallenged by the outside world, it inevitably decays.

Art, Annihilation, and the Abyss Within

One of the most fascinating aspects of *The Fall of the House of Usher* is its exploration of art and aesthetic experience as both a refuge and a reflection of madness. Roderick is a painter, a poet, and a musician. He surrounds himself with artistic creations that are beautiful but unsettling—works that echo the unreality of his experience. He plays eerie music, paints abstract landscapes, and recites a haunting poem, "The Haunted Palace," which serves as an allegory for the story itself. The poem describes a palace once glorious, now invaded by "evil things, in robes of sorrow." The palace, like the house, is a metaphor for the mind—once noble, now overrun by darkness.

For Poe, art is not separate from life, but a mirror of it. Roderick's art reflects his unraveling. The very act of creation becomes a form of confession, a way of externalizing the internal collapse. But it is not redemptive. There is no healing in Roderick's art—only a deeper plunge into horror. His aesthetic sensitivity becomes a curse, heightening his susceptibility to madness and linking his fate to the very structure he inhabits.

This connection between mind and environment, between art and reality, leads to the story's final revelation: the return of Madeline and the literal fall of the house. Her reappearance is not just a moment of shock—it is the return of the repressed, the surfacing of what Roderick tried to bury, both literally and psychologically. When she collapses into his arms, the twins die together, and the house, symbolically and physically, crumbles into the tarn.

The narrator escapes, but not unchanged. He flees into the night, watching as the "red moon" lights the final destruction. The story ends not with resolution but with annihilation. Everything—house, family, history—is gone. The abyss has swallowed it whole. Poe, true to his themes, leaves us with the unsettling knowledge that beneath the surface of reason and order lies a chasm of fear, madness, and death.

Yet this annihilation is not meaningless. It is a journey into the limits of human experience, a confrontation with the unknown that art alone can make bearable. Poe's genius lies in his ability to give form to the formless—to write fear into being, to chart the contours of collapse with poetic precision. *The Fall of the House of Usher* is not just a horror story—it is a masterpiece of literary architecture, a carefully constructed descent into dread that echoes long after the final sentence.

As you enter the halls of the Usher estate, prepare to leave behind the rational world. This is a place where walls breathe, portraits watch, and silence speaks. Where death is not final, and the mind is its own haunted house. Poe will not guide you safely out. He offers no lantern, no exorcism, no happy ending. Only the lingering echo of a voice, the shudder of recognition, and the realization that what has fallen may still be falling—within us all.

The Fall of
The House of Usher

Throughout an entire dull, dark, and silent day in autumn, when the clouds hung heavily and oppressively low in the sky, I had been traveling alone on horseback through a particularly dreary stretch of countryside, and finally found myself, as evening shadows began to fall, within sight of the gloomy House of Usher. I don't know how it happened— but with my first glimpse of the building, a sense of unbearable gloom filled my entire being. I say unbearable because the feeling wasn't softened by any of that half-pleasant, poetic sentiment that the mind usually experiences even when viewing the harshest natural scenes of desolation or terror. I looked at the scene before me—at the house itself, and the simple landscape features of the property—at the stark walls—at the empty, eye-like windows—at some wild sedges—and at several white trunks of rotting trees— with a complete depression of soul that I can only compare to the after-effects of an opium user's dream—the bitter return to everyday life—the horrible falling away of illusion. There was a coldness, a sinking feeling, a nauseating of the heart—an unredeemed bleakness of thought that no prodding of the imagination could transform into anything sublime. What was it—I stopped to consider—what was it that so disturbed me about looking at the House of Usher? It was a completely unsolvable mystery, and I couldn't wrestle with the vague fantasies that flooded my mind as I thought about it. I was forced to settle on the unsatisfying conclusion that while there are undoubtedly combinations of very simple natural objects that have the power to affect us this way, the analysis of this power lies beyond our understanding. It was possible, I thought, that simply rearranging the elements of the scene, the details of the picture, would be enough to change, or perhaps completely destroy its ability to create such a sorrowful impression; and acting on this idea, I guided my horse to the steep edge of a black and ominous pool that lay in undisturbed brightness beside the house, and looked down—but with an even more intense shudder than before—at the altered and upside-down reflections of the gray sedge, the ghostly tree trunks, and the empty, eye-like windows.

Despite this, I decided to stay in this dark and gloomy house for several weeks. The owner, Roderick Usher, had been one of my close friends during childhood, but many years had passed since we last saw each other. Recently, however, I had received a letter from him while I was in a remote part of the country—a letter that was so desperately urgent in tone that it demanded nothing less than a face-to-face response. The handwritten document showed clear signs of nervous distress. The writer described severe physical illness—along with a mental condition that was weighing heavily on him—and expressed a sincere wish to see me, as his closest and truly his only personal friend, hoping that the uplifting nature of my companionship might provide some relief from his suffering. It was the way he expressed all of this, and so much more—it was the genuine emotion that accompanied his plea—that left me with no choice but to agree; and so I immediately responded to what I still thought was a very unusual request.

Although we had been close friends as boys, I really knew very little about my companion. He had always been extremely and habitually reserved. I was aware, however, that his very old family had been known for generations for a particular emotional sensitivity, which had expressed itself over many centuries in numerous works of exceptional art, and had shown itself more recently in repeated acts of generous but modest charity, as well as in a passionate dedication to the complexities, perhaps even more than to the conventional and easily recognized beauties, of musical knowledge. I had also learned the very striking fact that the lineage of the Usher family, ancient as it was, had never produced any lasting branches at any time; in other words, the entire family existed in a direct line of descent, and had always, with very minor and very brief exceptions, remained so. It was this lack, I thought, while considering how perfectly the character of the property matched the established character of the people, and while wondering about the possible influence that one might have had on the other over the long passage of centuries—it was this lack, perhaps, of relatives in side branches, and the resulting unchanging passing down from father to son of both the inheritance and the name, which had eventually so connected the two as to blend the original title of the property into the strange and ambiguous name of the "House of Usher"—a name which seemed to encompass, in the minds of the local people who used it, both the family and the family home.

I have said that the only result of my rather childish experiment—looking down into the dark pool—was to intensify my initial strange impression. There's no question that becoming aware of my growing superstition—for what else should I call it?—mainly served to speed up that very growth. I have long understood this to be the contradictory nature of all feelings rooted in fear. Perhaps for this reason alone, when I lifted my gaze from the pool's reflection back to the house itself, a peculiar notion took hold in my mind—an idea so absurd that I mention it only to demonstrate the powerful intensity of the feelings that weighed upon me. I had so influenced my own imagination that I genuinely came to believe that around the entire mansion and its grounds hung an atmosphere unique to that place and its immediate surroundings—an atmosphere that bore no resemblance to ordinary air, but which had risen from the rotting trees, the gray walls, and the silent pool— a toxic and mysterious mist, heavy, slow-moving, barely visible, and the color of lead.

Shaking off what must have been a dream from my mind, I examined the building's actual appearance more carefully. Its main characteristic appeared to be extreme old age. The discoloration from countless years was extensive. Tiny fungi covered the entire exterior, hanging like a delicate tangled web from the roof edges. Yet all of this existed without any remarkable structural decay. No part of the stonework had collapsed, and there seemed to be a strange contradiction between the still perfect fitting of its components and the crumbling state of the individual stones. This reminded me greatly of the deceptive wholeness of old woodwork that has rotted for many years in some forgotten cellar, undisturbed by any outside air. Apart from this sign of widespread deterioration, however, the structure showed little evidence of being unstable. Perhaps a careful observer's eye might have noticed a barely visible crack that ran from the front roof of the building and made its way down the wall in a zigzag pattern until it disappeared into the dark waters of the small lake.

Observing these details, I crossed a brief causeway to reach the house. A waiting servant took my horse, and I passed through the Gothic archway of the entrance hall. A quietly moving valet then led me in silence through numerous dark and winding corridors as we made our way to his master's studio. Everything I saw along the route somehow added to the unclear feelings I've already described. The surroundings—the carved ceilings, the dark wall hangings, the black ebony floors, and the ghostly heraldic displays that clinked as I walked past—were all things I had known since childhood. Though I readily admitted how familiar everything appeared, I remained puzzled by how strange were the thoughts that these ordinary sights awakened in me. On one of the staircases, I encountered the family doctor. His face seemed to show a mixture of sly calculation and confusion. He greeted me nervously and continued on his way. The valet then opened a door and brought me into his master's presence.

The room I found myself in was extremely large and had a high ceiling. The windows were long, narrow, and came to a point at the top, positioned so far above the black oak floor that they couldn't be reached from inside. Weak rays of crimson light filtered through the latticed glass panes, providing just enough illumination to make out the larger objects nearby; however, my eyes couldn't penetrate the distant corners of the room or the recesses of the arched and decorated ceiling. Dark curtains draped the walls. The furniture throughout was abundant, uncomfortable, old-fashioned, and worn. Numerous books and musical instruments were scattered around, but they failed to bring any life to the setting. I felt as though I was breathing in an atmosphere of sadness. A mood of harsh, profound, and hopeless gloom hung over everything and filled the entire space.

When I walked in, Usher got up from a sofa where he had been lying stretched out full length, and he greeted me with an energetic warmth that seemed, at first, to have something of excessive friendliness about it—the forced effort of a bored man of society. However, one look at his face convinced me that he was completely sincere. We sat down, and for several moments, while he remained silent, I stared at him with a feeling that was half pity, half wonder. Certainly, no man had ever changed so drastically in such a short time as Roderick Usher had! I could barely bring myself to accept that the person sitting before me was the same companion from my early childhood. Still, his facial features had always been striking. He had a deathly pale complexion; eyes that were large, bright, and more luminous than anything I could compare them to; lips that were somewhat thin and very pale, but with an exceptionally beautiful shape; a nose with delicate Hebrew characteristics, but with nostrils that were unusually wide for such features; a well-formed chin that, in its lack of prominence, suggested a lack of moral strength; hair with a softness and fineness that was more than web-like—these features, along with an unusually large forehead above the temple area, created a face that would not be easily forgotten. Now, in the simple exaggeration of the dominant qualities of these features, and of the expression they typically conveyed, there was so much change that I questioned who I was speaking to. The now ghostly paleness of his skin, and the now extraordinary brightness of his eyes, startled and even amazed me more than anything else. His silky hair had also been allowed to grow without any care, and as it floated rather than fell around his face in its wild, gossamer-like texture, I could not, even when I tried, connect its elaborate appearance with any notion of ordinary humanity.

I immediately noticed something inconsistent and incoherent about my friend's behavior, and I quickly realized this stemmed from a series of weak and pointless attempts to overcome his habitual nervousness—an extreme state of anxious agitation. I had actually been somewhat prepared for this, both from his letter and from my memories of certain childhood characteristics, as well as from conclusions I had drawn about his unusual physical build and temperament. His behavior alternated between being lively and moody. His voice shifted rapidly from a shaky uncertainty (when his energy seemed completely drained) to a kind of forceful brevity—that sudden, weighty, unhurried, and hollow-sounding pronunciation—that heavy, perfectly balanced and controlled throaty speech that you might hear from a hopeless drunk or an incurable opium addict during their moments of most intense excitement.

This is how he spoke about the reason for my visit, his sincere desire to see me, and the comfort he hoped I would bring him. He went into considerable detail about what he believed was the nature of his illness. It was, he explained, a hereditary condition that ran in his family, something he had given up hope of curing—though he quickly added that it was simply a nervous disorder that would certainly pass in time. The condition manifested itself through a variety of abnormal sensations. Some of these symptoms, as he described them to me, both fascinated and confused me, though perhaps the language he used and his overall way of telling it influenced my reaction. He was tormented by an unhealthy oversensitivity of his senses; he could only tolerate the blandest of foods; he was able to wear clothing made only from specific fabrics; the scent of any flowers overwhelmed him; his eyes suffered pain from even the dimmest light; and only certain sounds—those produced by stringed instruments—failed to fill him with dread.

I found him completely enslaved by an unusual kind of terror. "I'm going to die," he said, "I must die from this terrible madness. This is how, and only how, I will be destroyed. I fear what's coming in the future, not because of what will happen, but because of what those events will lead to. I tremble at the thought of any incident, even the smallest one, that might affect this unbearable disturbance of my soul. I truly have no fear of danger itself, except for its ultimate consequence—terror. In this weakened, in this pitiful state, I feel that the time will eventually come when I must give up both life and sanity together, in some battle with the terrible phantom, FEAR."

I also learned, bit by bit through fragmented and unclear hints, about another strange aspect of his mental state. He was trapped by certain superstitious beliefs about the house where he lived, and from which he had never dared to leave for many years—beliefs about an influence whose supposed power was described in terms too vague to repeat here—an influence that certain peculiarities in the actual structure and materials of his family estate had, through years of endurance, he claimed, gained control over his spirit—an effect that the physical presence of the gray walls and towers, and of the dark pond that they all overlooked, had eventually created upon his moral and emotional well-being.

He confessed, though reluctantly, that much of the strange darkness that troubled him could be attributed to a more natural and tangible cause—the serious and prolonged illness of his dearly loved sister, who was clearly nearing death. She had been his only companion for many years and was his final remaining family member in the world. "When she dies," he said with a pain I will never forget, "it would leave me—hopeless and weak as I am—as the last surviving member of the ancient Usher family." As he spoke these words, Lady Madeline (as she was known) walked slowly through a distant part of the room and vanished without acknowledging that I was there. I watched her with complete amazement mixed with fear, though I couldn't explain why I felt this way. A feeling of numbness overwhelmed me as I followed her departing figure with my eyes. When a door finally shut behind her, I instinctively looked toward her brother's face with great interest, but he had covered his face with his hands. All I could see was that an unusual paleness had spread across his thin fingers, through which many emotional tears were flowing.

Madeline's illness had long puzzled her doctors. The strange symptoms included a persistent lack of emotion, a slow deterioration of her body, and occasional brief episodes that resembled a catatonic state. Until now, she had managed to resist her disease and hadn't been confined to bed permanently. However, on the evening I arrived at the house, she finally gave in to the devastating effects of her condition. Her brother told me that night, visibly shaken, that she had collapsed under the overwhelming force of whatever was destroying her. I realized that the brief glimpse I had caught of her would likely be my last—I would never see the lady again, at least not while she was still alive.

For several days afterward, neither Usher nor I spoke her name; and during this time I devoted myself to sincere efforts to ease my friend's depression. We painted and read together, or I listened, as though in a dream, to the wild improvisations of his expressive guitar. And so, as our growing intimacy allowed me deeper access into the depths of his soul, I came to understand more painfully the hopelessness of any attempt to lift the spirits of a mind from which darkness, like an inherent and active force, flowed out onto everything in the moral and physical world in one continuous stream of despair.

I will always carry with me memories of the many profound hours I spent alone with the master of the House of Usher. However, I would fail if I tried to explain the exact nature of the studies or activities he drew me into or guided me through. A fevered and deeply troubled imagination cast an eerie, sulfurous glow over everything. His lengthy improvised funeral songs will echo in my ears forever. Among other memories, I painfully recall a particular strange distortion and expansion of the haunting melody from Von Weber's final waltz. From the paintings that his complex mind dwelled upon, which developed stroke by stroke into an unsettling vagueness that made me shudder all the more intensely because I trembled without knowing why—from these paintings, as vivid as their images remain before me now, I would struggle in vain to capture more than a small fraction in mere written words. Through the complete simplicity and stark bareness of his compositions, he commanded and overwhelmed attention. If any human being ever painted a pure concept, that person was Roderick Usher. For me, at least, given the circumstances that surrounded me then, there emerged from the abstract creations that this melancholy artist managed to project onto his canvas an intensity of unbearable dread, the likes of which I had never experienced even when viewing the undeniably brilliant yet overly tangible fantasies of Fuseli.

One of my friend's dreamlike visions, which wasn't quite as purely abstract as his others, can be described in words, though only weakly. A small painting showed the inside of an enormously long rectangular vault or tunnel, with low walls that were smooth, white, and completely unbroken by any features or decorations. Certain additional details in the design effectively communicated the idea that this underground chamber was buried at an extraordinary depth beneath the earth's surface. No exit could be seen anywhere along its enormous length, and no torch or other artificial light source was visible; yet intense beams of light poured throughout the space, washing everything in an eerie and unsettling brilliance.

I just mentioned that diseased condition of the hearing nerve that made all music unbearable to the patient, except for certain sounds from stringed instruments. Perhaps it was the narrow boundaries he imposed on himself with the guitar that largely created the strange quality of his performances. However, the passionate ease of his spontaneous compositions couldn't be explained this way. They must have been—and indeed were—both in the musical notes and in the words of his wild fantasies (since he often accompanied himself with improvised rhyming verses), the product of that intense mental focus and concentration I mentioned earlier as something only visible during specific moments of extreme artificial stimulation. I easily remembered the words of one of these musical pieces. I was probably more deeply affected by it when he performed it because, in the hidden or mystical meaning beneath the surface, I thought I detected—for the first time—Usher's complete awareness that his noble mind was losing its grip on sanity. The poem, which was called "The Haunted Palace," went almost exactly, if not word for word, like this:

I.

In the greenest of our valleys,
By good angels tenanted,
Once a fair and stately palace—
Radiant palace—reared its head.
In the monarch Thought's dominion—
It stood there!
Never seraph spread a pinion
Over fabric half so fair.

II.

Banners yellow, glorious, golden,
On its roof did float and flow;
(This—all this—was in the olden
Time long ago);
And every gentle air that dallied,
In that sweet day,
Along the ramparts plumed and pallid,
A winged odor went away.

III.

Wanderers in that happy valley
Through two luminous windows saw
Spirits moving musically
To a lute's well-tunèd law;
Round about a throne, where sitting
(Porphyrogene!)
In state his glory well befitting,
The ruler of the realm was seen.

IV.

And all with pearl and ruby glowing
Was the fair palace door,
Through which came flowing, flowing, flowing
And sparkling evermore,
A troop of Echoes whose sweet duty
Was but to sing,
In voices of surpassing beauty,
The wit and wisdom of their king.

V.

But evil things, in robes of sorrow,
Assailed the monarch's high estate;
(Ah, let us mourn, for never morrow
Shall dawn upon him, desolate!)
And, round about his home, the glory
That blushed and bloomed
Is but a dim-remembered story
Of the old time entombed.

VI.

And travellers now within that valley,
Through the red-litten windows see
Vast forms that move fantastically
To a discordant melody;
While, like a rapid ghastly river,
Through the pale door,
A hideous throng rush out forever,
And laugh—but smile no more.

I clearly remember that ideas sparked by this ballad led us down a path of discussion that revealed one of Usher's beliefs, which I mention not because it was particularly original (since other people have held similar views), but because of how stubbornly he clung to it. This belief, in its basic form, was that all plant life possessed consciousness. However, in his troubled mind, this concept had taken on a bolder nature and extended, under specific circumstances, into the realm of non-living matter. I cannot find adequate words to convey the complete scope or passionate intensity of his conviction. This belief was linked (as I mentioned earlier) to the gray stones of his ancestral home. He believed the conditions for consciousness had been met here through the way these stones were positioned—in how they were arranged, as well as in the pattern of the numerous fungi that covered them, and the rotting trees that surrounded them—most importantly, in the long uninterrupted persistence of this arrangement, and in its reflection in the motionless waters of the small lake. The proof—the proof of this consciousness—could be observed, he claimed (and I shuddered when he said this), in the slow but inevitable formation of a unique atmosphere around the waters and walls. The outcome was evident, he continued, in that quiet yet persistent and frightening force that had shaped his family's fate for generations, and that had made him into what I saw before me—what he had become. Such beliefs require no commentary, and I will offer none.*

Our books—the books that had made up a significant part of the sick man's mental world for years—were, as you might expect, perfectly suited to this ghostly atmosphere. We spent hours studying works like Gresset's "Ververt et Chartreuse"; Machiavelli's "Belphegor"; Swedenborg's

"Heaven and Hell"; Holberg's "Subterranean Voyage of Nicholas Klimm"; the "Chiromancy" texts by Robert Flud, Jean D'Indaginé, and De la Chambre; Tieck's "Journey into the Blue Distance"; and Campanella's "City of the Sun". One book he particularly loved was a small octavo edition of the "Directorium Inquisitorium" by the Dominican Eymeric de Gironne; and there were sections in Pomponius Mela about the ancient African Satyrs and Œgipans that would hold Usher spellbound for hours at a time. His greatest pleasure, though, came from reading an extremely rare and fascinating book printed in quarto Gothic—a manual from a long-forgotten church—the Vigiliæ Mortuorum Secundum Chorum Ecclesiæ Maguntinæ.

I couldn't stop thinking about the strange, ritualistic nature of this work and how it might affect someone prone to melancholy, when one evening he suddenly told me that Lady Madeline had died. He announced his plan to preserve her body for two weeks in one of the many vaults built into the main walls of the house before burying her permanently. The practical reason he gave for this unusual decision was one I didn't feel I could argue against. Her brother had decided on this course of action, he explained to me, because of the strange nature of the deceased's illness, the persistent and intrusive questions from her doctors, and the isolated and vulnerable location of the family burial ground. I won't deny that when I remembered the menacing face of the person I had encountered on the staircase the day I arrived at the house, I had no wish to object to what I considered, at best, a harmless and perfectly reasonable precaution.

At Usher's request, I personally helped him with the arrangements for the temporary burial. After the body had been placed in a coffin, the two of us carried it alone to its resting place. The vault where we placed it (which had been closed for so long that our torches, nearly extinguished in its stifling atmosphere, gave us little chance to examine it properly) was small, damp, and completely without any way for light to enter; it lay deep underground, directly beneath the part of the building where my own bedroom was located. It had apparently been used in ancient feudal times for the darkest purposes of a dungeon keep, and in more recent years as a storage place for gunpowder or some other highly flammable material, since part of its floor and the entire interior of a long archway that led to it were carefully lined with copper. The door, made of heavy iron, had also been protected in the same way. Its enormous weight produced an unusually sharp, scraping sound as it turned on its hinges.

After placing our sorrowful burden on supports within this terrifying chamber, we partially pulled back the still-unfastened lid of the coffin and gazed upon the face of its occupant. A remarkable resemblance between the brother and sister suddenly caught my attention for the first time; and Usher, perhaps sensing my thoughts, whispered a few words that revealed the deceased and he had been twins, and that mysterious connections of an almost incomprehensible nature had always bound them together. Our eyes, however, did not linger long on the dead woman—for we could not look at her without feeling overwhelmed. The illness that had buried the lady in the prime of her youth had left behind, as is typical with all diseases of a purely cataleptic nature, the illusion of a pale flush on her chest and face, and that eerily persistent smile on her lips that is so frightening in death. We put the lid back in place and screwed it down, and after securing the iron door, we made our difficult way back to the barely less somber rooms in the upper part of the house.

After several days of intense sorrow had passed, a noticeable transformation occurred in my friend's mental condition. His usual behavior had disappeared. His regular activities were either ignored or completely forgotten. He wandered from room to room with quick, irregular, and purposeless steps. His face had grown even more deathly pale, if that was possible—but the brightness in his eyes had completely disappeared. The occasional roughness in his voice was no longer present; instead, a shaking tremor, as though he was extremely frightened, constantly marked his speech. There were moments when I believed his constantly troubled mind was struggling with some overwhelming secret, one he was fighting to find the courage to reveal. At other times, I had to conclude that these were simply the unexplainable peculiarities of insanity, as I watched him stare into empty space for hours at a time, sitting with the deepest concentration, as though he was listening to some sound that existed only in his imagination. It was hardly surprising that his condition frightened me—that it affected me as well. I could feel the strange power of his own bizarre yet compelling beliefs slowly but surely taking hold of me.

It was especially when I went to bed late on the night of the seventh or eighth day after Lady Madeline had been placed in the vault that I felt the full force of these emotions. Sleep wouldn't come to me—the hours passed slowly away. I tried to rationalize the anxiety that controlled me. I attempted to convince myself that much, if not all, of what I was experiencing came from the disturbing effect of the room's dark furniture—the black and worn curtains that were twisted into movement by the wind of a growing storm, swaying restlessly back and forth on the walls and rustling uneasily around the bed's decorations. But my efforts were useless. An uncontrollable shaking gradually spread through my body, and eventually, a nightmare of completely groundless fear settled on my heart. Throwing this off with a gasp and a struggle, I raised myself up on the pillows and, staring intently into the deep darkness of the room, listened—I don't know why, except that some instinctive feeling urged me—to certain quiet and unclear sounds that came through the breaks in the storm at long intervals from I didn't know where. Overwhelmed by an intense feeling of horror that was inexplicable yet unbearable, I quickly put on my clothes (because I knew I wouldn't sleep anymore that night) and tried to shake myself out of the pathetic state I had fallen into by walking rapidly back and forth across the room.

I had only walked back and forth a few times when I heard light footsteps on a nearby staircase that caught my attention. I immediately recognized them as Usher's. A moment later, he knocked gently on my door and came in, carrying a lamp. His face looked as pale as a corpse, as it always did—but there was also a kind of crazy cheerfulness in his eyes and what seemed like barely controlled hysteria in his entire manner. His appearance frightened me—but anything was better than the loneliness I had been suffering through for so long, and I actually welcomed his company as a relief.

"And you haven't seen it?" he said suddenly, after staring around him for several moments in silence—"you haven't seen it then?—but wait! you will." Speaking these words, and having carefully shielded his lamp, he rushed to one of the windows and threw it wide open to the storm.

The violent force of the rushing wind nearly knocked us off our feet. It was truly a stormy yet starkly beautiful night, one that was wildly unique in both its terror and its beauty. A whirlwind had apparently gathered its strength in our area, as there were frequent and violent changes in the wind's direction. The incredible thickness of the clouds, which hung so low they seemed to press down on the house's towers, didn't stop us from seeing the lifelike speed with which they raced from all directions, crashing into each other without disappearing into the distance. I say that even their incredible thickness didn't prevent us from seeing this—yet we caught no sight of the moon or stars, and there was no flash of lightning. But the bottom surfaces of the enormous masses of churning vapor, along with all the earthly objects right around us, were glowing in the unnatural light of a faintly glowing and clearly visible gaseous mist that hung around and covered the mansion.

"You must not—you cannot look at this!" I said, trembling, to Usher, as I guided him with firm gentleness away from the window to a chair. "These strange sights that are confusing you are simply electrical phenomena that happen quite often—or perhaps they come from the foul vapors rising from the pond. Let's close this window—the air is cold and harmful to your health. Here's one of your favorite novels. I'll read aloud, and you can listen—this way we'll get through this awful night together."

The old book I had picked up was the "Mad Trist" by Sir Launcelot Canning; but I had called it one of Usher's favorites more as a bitter joke than seriously; for, honestly, there was little in its crude and unimaginative wordiness that could have interested my friend's elevated and spiritual nature. It was, however, the only book within reach; and I held onto a faint hope that the agitation which now disturbed this melancholy man might find some relief (since the study of mental illness is filled with such strange contradictions) even in the complete absurdity of what I was about to read. If I could have judged by the wild, excessive energy with which he listened, or seemed to listen, to the words of the story, I might well have celebrated the success of my plan.

I had reached that famous part of the story where Ethelred, the hero of the Trist, having tried unsuccessfully to gain peaceful entry into the hermit's home, decides to force his way inside. Here, as you'll recall, the story reads as follows:

"And Ethelred, who was naturally brave-hearted, and who was now especially powerful because of the strength of the wine he had drunk, waited no longer to negotiate with the hermit, who was truly stubborn and spiteful by nature, but, feeling the rain on his shoulders, and fearing the approaching storm, raised his club immediately, and, with heavy strikes, quickly made space in the wooden planks of the door for his armored hand; and now pulling with great force, he cracked, split, and tore everything apart so completely, that the sound of the dry and hollow-echoing wood startled and rang throughout the forest."

When I finished reading that sentence, I stopped suddenly and paused for a moment. It seemed to me—though I immediately decided that my overexcited imagination was playing tricks on me—that from somewhere deep within the house, I could faintly hear what sounded exactly like an echo of the same cracking and tearing noise that Sir Launcelot had described in such detail. The echo was muffled and dull, but unmistakable. Without question, it was simply the coincidence that caught my attention. After all, with the windows rattling in their frames and all the usual sounds of the growing storm, there was nothing about the noise itself that should have concerned or upset me. I continued reading the story:

"But the brave champion Ethelred, now entering through the door, was deeply angered and astonished to find no trace of the evil hermit; but instead, a dragon of enormous and scaly appearance, with a fiery tongue, which sat guarding a palace of gold with a floor of silver; and upon the wall there hung a shield of gleaming brass with this inscription written upon it—"

> Who entereth herein, a conqueror hath bin;
> Who slayeth the dragon, the shield he shall win.
> Ethelred raised his mace and struck the dragon's head,
> causing it to fall before him and release its foul breath
> with a shriek so horrible and harsh, and so piercing,
> that Ethelred had to cover his ears with his hands
> against the terrible noise,
> the likes of which had never been heard before.

Here I stopped suddenly once more, this time filled with wild astonishment—because there was absolutely no question that I actually did hear (though I couldn't determine where it was coming from) a quiet and seemingly far-off, yet rough, drawn-out, and extremely strange screaming or scraping noise—the precise match of what my imagination had already created for the dragon's supernatural cry as the storyteller had described it.

Overwhelmed as I certainly was by this second and most extraordinary coincidence, experiencing a thousand conflicting emotions where amazement and intense fear dominated, I still managed to keep enough composure to avoid drawing attention to my companion's delicate nervousness through any comment. I wasn't entirely sure he had heard the sounds I was referring to, though there had definitely been a strange change in his behavior over the past few minutes. He had gradually turned his chair from its original position facing mine so that he now sat looking toward the chamber door, which meant I could only see part of his face, though I noticed his lips were shaking as if he were whispering something I couldn't hear. His head had fallen forward onto his chest, but I knew he wasn't sleeping because when I glimpsed his eye in profile, it was wide open and staring rigidly. His body movements also contradicted the idea that he was asleep, as he swayed gently but continuously from side to side in a steady, rhythmic motion. After quickly observing all of this, I returned to the story of Sir Launcelot, which continued as follows:

"And now, the champion, having escaped from the terrible rage of the dragon, remembering the bronze shield and the breaking of the spell that was cast upon it, moved the dead body out of his path and courageously approached across the silver floor of the castle to where the shield hung upon the wall; which indeed did not wait for him to reach it completely, but fell down at his feet onto the silver floor with an enormously loud and terrifying ringing sound."

As soon as those words left my mouth, I heard a distinct, hollow, metallic, and clanging sound that seemed muffled, as if a brass shield had just crashed heavily onto a silver floor. Completely shaken, I jumped to my feet, but Usher's steady rocking motion remained undisturbed. I rushed over to the chair where he was sitting. His eyes stared straight ahead, fixed and unblinking, and his entire face showed a stone-like stiffness. However, when I put my hand on his shoulder, his whole body trembled violently; a sickly smile flickered across his lips; and I could see that he was speaking in a low, rushed, and incoherent mumble, as though he wasn't aware I was there. Leaning in close to him, I finally understood the terrible meaning of what he was saying.

"Don't you hear it?—yes, I hear it, and I've been hearing it. For a long—long—long time—many minutes, many hours, many days, I've been hearing it—yet I didn't dare—oh, have pity on me, miserable wretch that I am!—I didn't dare—I didn't dare speak! We buried her alive in the tomb! Didn't I tell you that my senses were sharp? I'm telling you now that I heard her first weak movements in the hollow coffin. I heard them—many, many days ago—yet I didn't dare—I didn't dare speak! And now—tonight—Ethelred—ha! ha!—the breaking of the hermit's door, and the death-cry of the dragon, and the clashing of the shield!—say, rather, the splitting of her coffin, and the scraping of the iron hinges of her prison, and her struggles within the copper-lined archway of the vault! Oh! Where can I escape to? Won't she be here soon? Isn't she hurrying to scold me for my haste? Haven't I heard her footstep on the stair? Don't I recognize that heavy and horrible beating of her heart? Madman!"—here he jumped furiously to his feet, and screamed out his words, as if in the effort he were giving up his soul—"Madman! I tell you that she now stands outside the door!"

As if his words carried supernatural power and cast some kind of spell, the massive old doors he had pointed to immediately began to swing open slowly, their heavy black panels creaking apart. The rushing wind had pushed them open—but standing beyond those doors was the tall, shrouded figure of Lady Madeline of Usher. Blood stained her white clothing, and every part of her wasted body showed signs of a terrible struggle. She stood there for a moment, shaking and swaying back and forth in the doorway—then, letting out a low, mournful cry, she collapsed heavily onto her brother, and in her violent final death throes, she dragged him down to the floor as a corpse, a victim of the very horrors he had been dreading.

I fled from that room and from that house in terror. The storm was still raging with full fury as I found myself crossing the old stone bridge. Suddenly a strange light streaked along the path, and I turned to see where such an unusual glow could have come from, since only the enormous house and its shadows lay behind me. The brightness came from the full, setting, blood-red moon that now blazed clearly through that crack I had mentioned earlier—the one that was once barely visible, running in a zigzag pattern from the roof of the building down to its foundation. As I stared, this crack quickly grew wider—a violent gust of wind swept through—the entire moon suddenly burst into full view—my mind spun as I watched the massive walls splitting apart—there came a long, chaotic roaring sound like the voice of a thousand rushing waters—and the deep, dark pond at my feet closed gloomily and quietly over the ruins of the "House of Usher."

THE END

Thank You For Reading

You've Just Read a Piece of the Greatest Library Ever Rebuilt

Thank you for reading.

This book is one of thousands we're restoring, reimagining, and translating as part of the **Modern Library of Alexandria** — a global movement to preserve and share humanity's most important ideas.

What was once lost to fire and time is now rising again — not just as memory, but as living, breathing knowledge, freely accessible to all.

What You Can Do Next:

- **Keep Reading.**

  Discover more legendary works — in beautiful print, audiobook, or digital form — at LibraryofAlexandria.com.

- **Build Your Own Library.**

  Every title is available as a paperback, hardcover, or collectible boxset — at true printing cost. Craft a personal library worthy of display.

- **Spread the Light.**

  Share this book. Tell others about the movement. Help us translate every timeless work into every language, so no reader is ever left behind.

By finishing this book, you've already taken part in something extraordinary.

Join us at LibraryofAlexandria.com

Together, we're rebuilding the greatest library the world has ever known.

With appreciation,

The Modern Library of Alexandria Team

Visit:
www.libraryofalexandria.com
Or scan the code below: